Happiness: Is happiness the purpose of life?

Editorial

Is happiness the purpose of life? That must depend on what you mean by happiness. And purpose. And perhaps life! Having asked many students, 11–18s, over the last few years, it certainly features in their goals for life, even if they can't articulate quite what they mean.

But perhaps we shouldn't be pursuing happiness at all – once we start asking ourselves if we are happy, it eludes us. As Calvin (the cartoon boy by Bill Watterson rather than the sixteenth-century Protestant theologian) once said: 'Here I am, happy and content … but not euphoric. So now I'm no longer content. My day is ruined. I need to stop thinking while I'm ahead.' Perhaps it is better to see happiness as the side-effect of a virtuous life rather than a goal. Or perhaps we shouldn't be bothering with happiness at all. Rabbi David Blumenthal comments, 'It is caring, not inner peace or contentment that counts. If caring makes us happy, great; if not, so what? We still need to care.'

Happiness is a complex word, intuitively understood by all but open to many different interpretations. In one form or another, it can be applied to the routine experiences of day-to-day living and also a state of ultimate, eternal bliss. Where people reject the idea of an afterlife, happiness in this life is a desirable aim. From popular psychology to economics to politics, happiness is seen as an acceptable secular goal.

This book wrestles with the concept of happiness, the question of how to get it and, indeed, if one should aim to be happy. What kind of happiness is offered in the Bible (see pp.4–9) or in Buddhism (pp.10–15)? How can we respond when suffering destroys happiness (pp.18–23)? And what impact does seeking the 'greatest happiness for the greatest number' have on living (pp.24–29)? In the process, students get opportunities to reflect upon their own understanding and consider the extent to which religious and secular responses illuminate their thinking.

Stephen Pett
Editor

Contents

Page	Section	Age range
2	**Getting started: eight ways to introduce a unit on happiness** Stephen Pett	11–16
4	**What can the Bible teach us about happiness? Should we listen?** Stephen Pett	11–13
10	**What does Buddhism teach about happiness?** Fiona Moss and Stephen Pett	11–14
16	**Topical film: using *Africa United*** Stephen Pett	12–14
18	**What do we do when unhappiness comes? Exploring the Book of Job** Lat Blaylock	13–16
24	**Is happiness the same as pleasure? Applying ethical hedonism** Kate Christopher	14–16
30	**Topical artefact: Happiness jars** Stephen Pett	11–16
32	**Entry-level and extension activities** Lat Blaylock and Stephen Pett	11–16

RE Today Services

Getting started
Eight ways to introduce a unit on happiness

1 What on earth is happiness?

It is good to think about what we mean by the term, so some simple definitions are useful.

Start by asking students for their ideas of what happiness is and what they think might bring happiness. Ask students to bring in images and/or music as a prompt for this. Reflecting on the second question might illuminate responses to the first, so explore both together.

To get beyond suggestions of material goods that students might start with, give them a series of headings: what makes you happy at home, at school, with friends, about the world, inside (your mind, heart, 'spirit'), and one other.

Ask students to draw a target-board with happiness at the centre. Get them to place the things that are most important for happiness near the centre, and things that have little impact or relevance further away.

Compare their ideas of what is most and least important.

2 Are there different ways of understanding happiness?

Following on from Activity 1, ask students to analyse the class's responses to what brings happiness. Can they sort them into categories? What are the categories? You might suggest that how long the happiness lasts, or how much impact it has, or whether it copes with difficulty and suffering could be interesting ways of categorising.

Compare your students' categories with the following ideas:

Is happiness something to do with:

- overall satisfaction with the way life is going/has gone
- emotion
- flourishing in life
- having a sense of purpose
- pleasure
- the transcendent – beyond the material world? (Five of these are explored further on p.33.)

Consider whether there is a hierarchy here – are some types of happiness more enduring or better than others? Which ones and why?

3 The experience machine

Ask your students:

> **Suppose there were an experience machine that could give you any experience you desired.** Super-duper neuropsychologists could stimulate your brain so that you would think and feel you were writing a great novel, or making a friend, or reading an interesting book. All the time you would be floating in a tank, with electrodes attached to your brain. Should you plug into this machine for life, pre-programming your life's experiences?
>
> Robert Nozick, *Anarchy, State and Utopia*, Wiley 1978

If you could be plugged into a machine in which you would feel continually happy, enjoying highly pleasurable experiences and feeling profoundly satisfied, would you want to be plugged in?

Nozick argues that we would not want to go into the machine. We want to *do* certain things, not just believe we are doing them. We want to *be* a certain way, *be* a certain sort of person. We want life and living to be *real*.

'Plugging into the machine is a kind of suicide,' he says. Is there more to happiness than feeling happy? Is there more to life than happiness?

4 Choices, choices

Ask students to respond to these choices about happiness and life. You might give them a continuum line if you want to allow subtleties, or just an either/or choice – plus reasons.

- Is it better to live for pleasure or to seek a meaningful life?
- Is it better to try and hang on to happy experiences or to let them go?
- Is it better to be wise and unhappy, or happy and stupid?
- Is it better to be rich and miserable or poor and happy?
- Is it better to have bursts of ecstasy occasionally in a fairly tedious life, or a basically reasonably humdrum life without ecstasy?
- Is it better to suffer in this life with eternal happiness to come, or have comfort now, with no afterlife?
- Is it better to suffer here with eternal happiness to come, or *to suffer* here, with no afterlife?
- Is it better to suffer here *with the hope of* eternal happiness, or to suffer here with no hope of eternal happiness?

5 Creating a happy world

Scottish Philosopher David Hume suggested that perhaps the best we might infer from the current world was that it was the 'first rude essay of some infant deity who afterwards abandoned it, ashamed of his lame performance' (*Dialogues Concerning Natural Religion*, 1779). Can your students do any better?

Ask students to imagine that there really is a god. God wants the world to be happy. What kind of world would he create?

Ask students to offer their five 'divine fixes' to upgrade Life's Operating System 1.0 to LOS 2.0.

What features of the current natural world would remain? What aspects of current society would be kept? What aspects of human nature would change? What are the implications of any changes? For example, removing pain might prevent us noticing physical harm; making everything pleasurable might flatten out all experiences.

Students might need to decide if they see happiness as about pleasure, emotion or something else, and whether unhappiness has any value, and if so, how much.

6 What in heaven is happiness?

If an afterlife is meant to make up for unhappiness now, what must it be like? Ask students to speculate about 'heaven' (or its equivalent) for a hedonist, a spiritual agnostic, a Buddhist and a Christian.

Compare their ideas with the extracts below. What similarities and differences are there? What questions do students have?

> In Roman Catholic theology, the Beatific Vision, a perfect and permanent state, includes the sight or vision of God, the love of God, … and the enjoyment of God, an act of excessive joy, by which the soul rejoices in the possession of God, and in the enjoyment of Him a soul's cravings for happiness are completely gratified.
>
> Adapted from F J Boudreaux, SJ, *The Happiness of Heaven*, Tredition 2012

> Not like this world is the World to Come …[where] there is neither eating nor drinking; no procreation of children or business transactions; no envy or hatred or rivalry; but the righteous sit enthroned, their crowns on their heads, and enjoy the lustre of the Divine Splendour (*Shechinah*)
>
> Judaism: Talmud, Berakot 17a

> In this Pure Land … all wishes those beings may think of, they will be fulfilled, as long as they are rightful.
>
> Buddhism: read the beautiful description in the larger Sukhavativyuha Sutra 15–18
> http://bit.ly/1DdvlDA

7 Art gallery

An A5 copy of the cover art can be found on the back cover, ready to copy and enlarge to A4. Alternatively, members can download a copy from the website.

Ask students to imagine that an art gallery is putting on an exhibition entitled 'Happiness, Religion and Belief'. Ask students to take images from the cover art and write a short description and explanation of each for the exhibition. They should give the image a title and explain how it relates to the theme of the exhibition, noting the links to religion and belief.

What other images should be included? Ask students to find at least three more images to include – video images, songs or objects can all be considered for inclusion. They need to write their exhibition labels for these extra items too.

8 Happiness as your secret motive?

American psychologist and philosopher William James said, 'How to gain, how to keep, how to recover happiness, is in fact for most [human beings] at all times the secret motive of all they do, and of all they are willing to endure.' (*Varieties of Religious Experience*, 1902).

a In pairs or groups, take the images from the cover and rank them in order of how much students think people would be prepared to endure for this kind of happiness (e.g. is the desire for eternal happiness greater than the desire for a burger …? Why?)

b Which image reflects religious commitment best? Would a believer endure more than someone without religious belief? Why/why not?

c Ask students to take two from the top and one from the bottom of this ranking and talk about how much they would endure for this happiness and why?

What can the Bible teach us about happiness? Should we listen?

Overview

If you ask students what their goal in life is, many will respond that it is to be happy. Of course, you might then go on to ask what they mean by 'happy'! Routes to happiness are worth exploring in RE, not least because all religions have something to say about what it is that brings a rich, enjoyable, fulfilling and meaningful life – all of which are arguably components of happiness. This unit explores some routes to happiness from the Bible, comparing them to findings from contemporary positive psychology. It thus enables students to reflect upon the relationship between ancient and modern teachings, and evaluate whether there is wisdom in either.

Essential knowledge

There is not a great deal about happiness in the Bible. It is clear that it is not a self-help manual for those seeking quick steps to happiness: following God's path is costly (e.g. Jesus says, 'If anyone would come after me, let him deny himself and take up his cross and follow me' – Matthew 16:24). However, the Bible does suggest that there is something deeper than a passing emotion that is available to those who love God and love their neighbour. The Bible uses the term *asrey (ashrey)* in the Old Testament and *makarios* in the New Testament. Both can be translated as 'happy', although many translations use the word 'blessed' instead. This is perhaps to indicate that happiness is something to be seen as a gift from God, rather than a human prerogative.

The Bible demands a life of love for God and for neighbour, exemplified for Christians in the life and teaching of Jesus. The virtuous Christian life of love, charity, service, humility, generosity and thanksgiving is seen as a response of gratitude and obedience, rather than as a path to happiness in this life. However, it is part of a longer-term goal of being united with God after death, which is seen as perfect happiness (e.g. Colossians 3: 1–17).

Recent research in psychology has shown the positive impact of the virtuous life, regardless of one's religious beliefs. Many of the suggested steps to happiness offered as a result of positive psychology research seem to reflect the ways of behaving encouraged in religion. These range from attitudes to pleasure through to having a sense of purpose in life. The psychology research does not confirm the *truth* or otherwise of religious beliefs, but it does offer something to explore as to the *value* of religious practice.

Of course, all these virtues represent an ideal of Christian living – most Christians would be the first to admit that they fail to live up to these exacting standards.

Essential teaching and learning

This unit requires students to learn about Christian and secular ideas to do with happiness, to speculate, compare similarities and differences between viewpoints, interpret and analyse a range of texts, evaluate different approaches to happiness, apply their learning to problems and express their ideas in a range of ways. It enables students to engage in thoughtful questioning, processing ideas and coming to (perhaps tentative) conclusions.

11–13

Context

This unit is a good way of exploring the impact of belief on a Christian's life. It would fit well as part of a systematic study of Christian living.

Resources/links

Most of the evidence from psychology research can be found in Stephen Post and Jill Neimark, *Why Good Things Happen to Good People*, Broadway 2008: http://unlimitedloveinstitute.org/

More detailed academic papers are found in CJ Snyder and SJ Lopez (eds), *The Handbook of Positive Psychology* (OUP 2005), and S David, I Boniwell and A C Ayers (eds) *Oxford Handbook of Happiness* (OUP 2014).

Online magazine *Aeon* regularly has fascinating and thoughtful articles and short videos that are useful in RE. For example, this one on the effectiveness of classes for forgiveness: http://bit.ly/1wjsQrT

More on forgiveness at: http://theforgivenessproject.com/

More ideas for exploring happiness in religion and secular life can be found in the section 'Is Happiness the purpose of life?' in Stephen Pett (ed.), *Questions: Meaning, Purpose and Truth* (RE Today 2012).

Learning activities

1 What kinds of actions lead to happiness?

You might prepare for this unit by getting students to choose one soap opera or drama and watch an episode in advance. Ask them to identify actions and behaviour that lead characters to happiness and unhappiness. Compare the results and discuss what actions seem to result in most happiness. Can students add insights from their own experiences?

2 From where can we get wise advice on happiness?

a Ask students in groups to speculate on what they think the Bible might say about what brings happiness. What kinds of actions do they expect the Bible to encourage? Give students a copy of p.6. In pairs, ideally cutting and sticking onto an A3 sheet, match the summaries and the supporting biblical texts. Compare students' ideas with these. Are there any surprises? Compare with their responses from Activity 1. Discuss: How far does the Bible offer any wise advice for people who are not Christians?

b Page 7 gives some of the findings from contemporary research in the field of positive psychology. Ask students to compare with the advice in the Bible. They can try and match the psychology with the biblical advice (for example, cutting them out and sticking them onto the A3 sheet from (a) above), saying what similarities and differences there are. Are there any surprises? Discuss: How far does the psychology offer wise advice?

3 What are the effects of being happy?

a Page 8 offers a range of descriptions of a happy life from the Bible. Ask students to find or sketch images to illustrate two of the descriptions, annotating them to explain how they reflect the biblical idea and how a Christian might attain this happy life.

b Ask students to devise a metaphor or image for a flourishing, happy secular society, building on their learning and the information from psychology. This need not exclude religious ideas, of course. (You might compare these with some more 'recipes for happiness' found on p.15.)

4 Happiness: blessing or luck?

Tell students that the word *asrey* in the Bible is often translated as 'Blessed'. The word 'happiness' in English is linked to the word 'happen', linked with luck, fortune and chance. Return to some of the soap opera characters in Activity 1. Take a few examples and ask students to suggest how the character might behave differently if he or she believed happiness is a blessing from God, or a matter of chance, or something you can pursue for yourself.

5 Should Christians be happier than non-Christians?

Give students the statement: 'Christians ought to be happier than non-Christians.' From their studies in this unit, how might someone argue for this statement? You might debate this formally, or ask students to write a structured response. Page 9 offers a writing frame with a range of sentence starters. Good answers will use evidence and quotation from the sources studied.

6 Is this advice worth listening to?

Ask students to reflect: What are the steps for happiness offered by the Bible and psychology? Should they listen? What things that students do bring or block happiness? Is there anything they could do differently?

A personal response will draw upon their learning from these activities, perhaps offering three steps and a warning for how they live this year.

Outcomes

Students can demonstrate achievement at levels 4–6 in these activities if they can say 'yes' to some of these 'I can' statements.

Description of achievement

I can …

Level 4

- outline what the Bible and positive psychology have to say about how to be happy, making links between them

- compare these suggestions with my own ideas

Level 5

- explain how following the Bible's teachings or the research from positive psychology might make someone happy

- express my own ideas about what is challenging about aiming for happiness, in the light of my learning about Christianity and positive psychology

Level 6

- interpret biblical and secular sources to explain whether or not Christians should be happier than non-Christians, expressing my own insights.

This unit helps students in Scotland to achieve RME 3-09a and 3-09b.

Note: The levels used in the Outcomes column have been derived from the 2004 *Non-statutory National Framework for RE*. These are still found extensively in agreed syllabuses in England, but teachers are advised to consult the statutory requirements applicable to their school, as assessment processes change.

What leads to happiness? Advice from the Bible

Match the eight summaries on the left with the Bible texts that illustrate them on the right.

Summaries	Bible texts
Caring about others is central to Christian teaching, and it leads to happiness.	Happy are all who take refuge in God. *Psalm 2:12 (NRSV)* Happy are those who respect the LORD, who want what he commands. *Psalm 112.1 (NCV)*
Being thankful to God and saying it regularly to God in prayer. Appreciating the good things God has done, even when life gets tough.	Happy are the people who know how to praise you … *Psalm 89:16 (NCV)* Always be joyful. Pray continually, and give thanks whatever happens. *1 Thessalonians 5:16–18 (NCV)*
Having a future hope is central to a Christian. Life is not always about feeling happy, but hope of heaven outweighs the trials of life, keeping a sense of perspective.	Happy is the person whose sins are forgiven, whose wrongs are pardoned. Happy is the person whom the LORD does not consider guilty and in whom there is nothing false. *Psalm 32:1–2 (NCV)*
Having God at the centre of life is key. Putting your desires in line with what God wants.	I have learned the secret of being happy at any time in everything that happens, when I have enough to eat and when I go hungry, when I have more than I need and when I do not have enough. I can do all things through Christ, because he gives me strength. *Philippians 4:12–13 (NCV)*
Saying sorry, being forgiven by God and forgiving others is important. Jesus said Christians should keep on forgiving others.	What do workers gain from their toil? … I know that there is nothing better for people than to be happy and to do good while they live. That each of them may eat and drink, and find satisfaction in all their toil – this is the gift of God. *Ecclesiastes 3:9–11 (NIVUK)*
Standing up for what is right is demanding but worthwhile.	Jesus said: 'Love the Lord your God … and … love your neighbour as yourself.' *Matthew 22:37–39 (NIVUK)* Happy are those who consider the poor. *Psalm 41:1 (NRSV)*
Trusting in Jesus through all circumstances – good and bad – brings happiness to the apostle Paul, a model for Christians.	Jesus said: Those who want to do right more than anything else are happy, because God will fully satisfy them. Those who show mercy to others are happy, because God will show mercy to them. Those who work to bring peace are happy, because God will call them his children. *Matthew 5:5–9 (NCV online)*
Working hard and doing good bring satisfaction, as God's gift.	Our light and momentary troubles are achieving for us an eternal glory that far outweighs them all. So we fix our eyes not on what is seen, but on what is unseen, since what is seen is temporary, but what is unseen is eternal. *2 Corinthians 4:16–18 (NIVUK)*

What leads to happiness? Some advice from positive psychology

Gratitude is a positive response to good things that happen. Just 15 minutes a day focusing on things to be thankful for can improve happiness. It can help to give a balanced perspective, since bad events usually have more impact on us than good ones. People who are grateful are more likely to help others.

Forgiveness is a positive response to bad things. Forgiveness is a great medicine: it can lift depression, reduce anger and boost your mood. Some places offer courses in forgiveness, as it is a skill that needs practising. It is worth it, as forgiving others has more impact than being forgiven.

Compassion is an emotional response when recognising other people's suffering, linked with a desire to help. It is said to lead to happiness because giving is actually more pleasurable than receiving. It reduces stress by getting us to focus on the needs of others more than ourselves, making connections with others. Some research suggests it can help us live longer.

A life of **meaning and purpose** is the most fulfilling form of the 'happy life', according to Martin Seligman. He says that positive psychology 'takes you through the countryside of pleasure … up into the high country of strength and virtue, and finally to the peaks of lasting fulfilment: meaning and purpose' (*Authentic Happiness*, 2002).

Selfless giving contributes to happiness. Research shows that neighbourhoods with the highest levels of volunteering had less crime, better schools and happier and healthier residents. Teenagers who volunteer do significantly better in many aspects of life than those who don't. Even doing chores around the house help you to be happier in the long run …!

Courage is the hallmark of people who change the world. People who are passionate about justice and prepared to stand up for what is right often demonstrate empathy and sensitivity to fairness. They often lead lives of joy, faith and charity towards others.

Humour contributes to happiness! Laughter decreases stress hormones and increases dopamine, the feel-good hormone in our bodies. Laughter is linked to healthier hearts, higher self-esteem and a sense of emotional wellbeing. One hundred laughs is the aerobic equivalent of 10 minutes on a rowing machine …!

Hope contributes to a sense of satisfaction with life. Hope is about having goals to achieve, but also the will or desire to reach these goals *and* different ways of achieving them. Hope is important to overcome obstacles. It is not just a feel-good emotion but an active motivation to achieve. Higher levels of hope enable people to handle pain better and to have more friends.

What does a happy life look like? Images from the Bible

A happy person flourishes like a tree …

That person is like a tree planted by streams of water,
 which yields its fruit in season
and whose leaf does not wither –
 whatever they do prospers (or thrives).

Psalm 1:3 (NIVUK)

A happy person is fruitful …

The fruit of the Spirit is love, joy, peace, patience, kindness, goodness, faithfulness, gentleness and self-control. Against such things there is no law.

Galatians 5:22–23 (NIVUK)

A happy person will find rest, wholeness, contentment and peace (*shalom*)

(A picture from the Old Testament)
[The LORD says:]
Behold, I will create
new heavens and a new earth.
The sound of weeping and of crying
will be heard in it no more.
Never again will there be in it
an infant who only lives for a few days,
or an old man who does not live out his years;
he who dies at a hundred
will be thought a mere youth;
he who fails to reach a hundred
will be considered cursed.
They will build houses and dwell in them;
they will plant vineyards and eat their fruit.
No longer will they build houses
and others live in them,
or plant and others eat.
Every person will sit under their own vine
and under their own fig tree,
and no one will make them afraid,
for the LORD Almighty has spoken.

Adapted from Isaiah 65 and Micah 4

A happy life will be with God, in heaven

(A picture from the New Testament)

Then I [John] saw a new heaven and a new earth. The first heaven and the first earth disappeared, and the sea vanished. And I saw the Holy City, the new Jerusalem, coming down out of heaven from God, prepared and ready, like a bride dressed to meet her husband.

I heard a loud voice speaking from the throne: 'Now God's home is with human beings! He will live with them, and they shall be his people. God himself will be with them, and he will be their God. He will wipe away all tears from their eyes. There will be no more death, no more grief or crying or pain. The old things have disappeared.' Then the one who sits on the throne said, 'And now I make all things new!' …

The angel also showed me the river of the water of life, sparkling like crystal, and coming from the throne of God and of the Lamb and flowing down the middle of the city's street. On each side of the river was the tree of life, which bears fruit twelve times a year, once each month; and its leaves are for the healing of the nations. …The throne of God and of the Lamb will be in the city, and his servants will worship him. They will see his face, and his name will be written on their foreheads. There shall be no more night, and they will not need lamps or sunlight, because the Lord God will be their light, and they will rule as kings for ever and ever.

Adapted from Revelation 21 and 22 (GNB)

Should Christians be happier than non-Christians?

Below is a writing frame to help you present an argument, with evidence, showing what you have learned about happiness in the Bible and in positive psychology.

Look at the title, then take some sentence starters to help you write a short piece in response. Choose at least six sentence starters (you can adapt them if you wish, or create your own), and at least one from each column, so that you can present different viewpoints.

'Christians should be happier than non-Christians.' Do you agree?

Show that you have thought about different points of view.

This essay is about happiness. This means …	Positive psychology aims to help people to be happier because …	I agree with the idea that Christians should be happier because …
Some examples of happiness might be …	Some of the ways of getting happier include …	I disagree with this because …
The Bible teaches that happiness …		The most persuasive piece of advice is … because …
The Bible describes a happy life as …	These are similar to/different from the Bible's ideas in the following ways …	I am in a dilemma about …
Some of the actions that might lead to happiness include …	Believing in God may …	I do/do not think that happiness is important because …
The best idea is that …	The research from psychology suggests …	One thing I have learned about happiness from this studying it is …
One problem with this is …		I am not sure about …
Reasons why Christians should be happier than non-Christians include …	Reasons why non-Christians might/should be happier than Christians include …	I would like to think a bit more about …
Christians believe that all people are sinful and make mistakes, so …	The best thing about the research is that …	After all the arguments, I think …
The Christian community might help by …	On the other hand, a problem is …	One piece of advice I might try and put into practice in my life might be … because …

What does Buddhism teach about happiness?

Overview

Buddhism is sometimes characterised as a search for happiness. This unit explores this idea from the perspective of a British Tibetan nun. It allows students to build on their understanding of the Buddha's Four Sights, the Four Noble Truths and the Noble Eightfold Path and apply them to living in the UK today. The activities require careful study of the interview and offer different strategies to make sense of a Buddhist response to happiness, as well as considering the value of the insights to their own lives.

Essential knowledge

The teaching of the Buddha recognises that the current state of most people is one of discontentment, which the Buddha referred to as suffering. His teaching offers a way of removing this dissatisfaction or misery. The ultimate goal for most Buddhists is enlightenment, attaining nirvana/nibbana; some seek Buddhahood, where their goal is to bring enlightenment to all sentient beings. Along the way, following the teachings of the Buddha, many find happiness – perhaps described as a form of equanimity – where they are able to handle the good and the bad in life without being disturbed or distressed.

Buddhists believe that the Buddha discovered the truth about the nature of life and living, and that putting into practice his teachings (the Dharma/Dhamma) can lead to the liberation and the cessation of discontentment or suffering. This is not a temporary escape, as Venerable Choesang points out, but a state of living with complete equanimity.

Following the Buddha's path to liberation is the key, rather than a search for happiness itself, not least because good experiences pass, just as bad ones do. It is important that we do not focus on the moments of happiness and joy, nor the moments of pain and misery. Life is fleeting and we should not cling to it.

The Venerable Tsuiltrim Tenzin Choesang was ordained by His Holiness the 14th Dalai Lama of Tibet. Ani Choesang is a Gelongma, a fully ordained nun in the Tibetan tradition. She lives in Herefordshire and now mainly teaches in the UK and at her nunnery in Nepal.

Essential teaching and learning

This unit assumes that students have already encountered the key teachings of the Buddha and offers an opportunity to deepen their understanding of these core ideas. The question of happiness is of universal relevance to students, and close analysis of the interview allows them to apply their understanding of Buddhist teaching and practices, as well as to reflect on ideas of happiness for themselves. The final activity comparing a range of 'recipes for happiness' allows students to identify and explain similarities and differences between some religious and secular views.

11–14

Context

This work might be part of a systematic study of Buddhism, or part of a study on happiness across more than one religion. Before accessing this material, students will need to have an understanding of core Buddhist beliefs.

Resources/links

BBC Class Clips
Buddhist beliefs:
www.bbc.co.uk/education/clips/zmhkq6f

An introduction to Buddhist beliefs on suffering:
www.bbc.co.uk/education/clips/z3vq6sg

For resources on introducing the four sights, the Four Noble Truths and the Noble Eightfold Path, see Stephen Pett (ed.), *Questions: Buddhists* (RE Today 2012).

 Web: An extended version of this interview can be downloaded by NATRE members and *REtoday* subscribers from the subscribers' area of the website: www.retoday.org.uk

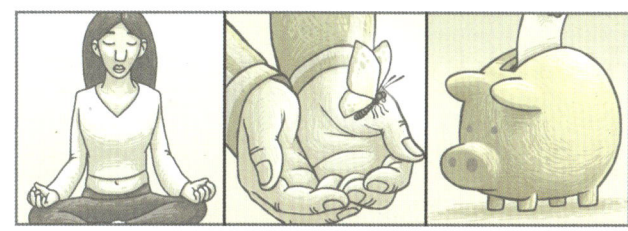

Learning activities

1 Filling the Karmic Piggy Bank

Introduce the students to Venerable Tsuiltrim Tenzin Choesang, a Tibetan Buddhist nun. Share her response to the question, 'What actions would lead a Buddhist to happiness?' on p.12.

Set up your class 'karmic piggy bank'. Give each student 2–3 pieces of paper and ask them to write an action that would be suitable to put in the karmic piggy bank. As they insert the actions into the piggy bank, ask them to justify why these thoughts and actions might work towards making a Buddhist happy.

2 Escaping dukkha/duknel

Share Venerable Choesang's response to the question 'Is happiness about escaping from Dukkha?' on p.12. The term dukkha is commonly translated as discontentment or suffering. (Tibetan Buddhists use the word *duknel* instead of dukkha.)

Using copies of p.14, ask the students to work in threes to come up with a real-life example for each of the three types of suffering, filling in column 1. Next, ask them to consider how each example might make a non-Buddhist feel, filling in column 3. As a class, in the light of their learning, discuss how a Buddhist might strive to take the Middle Way, reacting and behaving differently when faced with these examples of suffering. Record how a Buddhist might act or react to deal with suffering on the stepping stones in the middle of the page.

3 Analysing and interpreting an interview

Arrange the students into groups of four. Give each group a set of the remaining questions that were put to Venerable Choesang and the responses that she gave on p.13. Students should:

- match the questions to the responses from Venerable Choesang
- work in pairs to identify any difficult vocabulary and find meanings. This means one pair will have three responses to work with, and the other will have two.
- come back together as a four and discuss the questions and answers given by Venerable Choesang, sharing what they understand from her responses.

4 Creating a radio interview

In groups of four ask the students to recreate the interview with Venerable Choesang as if it was happening on a radio programme. Ask one student to be the interviewer. This person needs to prepare questions but also be prepared to act as a prompt or ask supplementary questions. The other three students need to prepare the responses given to the questions by Venerable Choesang, but using their own words, showing their understanding of the terms she used. Students then role-play the interview, taking it in turns to answer the questions.

Finally ask the students to write one paragraph as if they had been a listener to the radio interview, sharing what wisdom and insight they gained from Venerable Choesang that helped them.

5 The recipe for happiness

Share the selection of recipes for happiness and happiness quotes from p.15. Ask students to:

- write a short recipe for happiness that a Buddhist might write, from their learning
- write their own recipe for happiness
- write a comparison of the two recipes above, and one more from p.15, explaining and justifying the similarities and differences between the recipes, and reflecting on their impact on an individual and a community.

Outcomes

Students can demonstrate achievement at levels 4–6 in these activities if they can say 'yes' to some of these 'I can' statements.

Description of achievement

I can …

Level 4

- describe how following the teaching of the Buddha on dukkha, karma and the Middle Way might affect a Buddhist's day-to-day life.
- say what differences this approach to happiness might make to a community (e.g. school).

Level 5

- explain how following the teaching of the Buddha on dukkha, karma and the Middle Way might make a difference to the happiness of a Buddhist
- explain what might be challenging about following the Buddha's path to happiness in today's world.

Level 6

- interpret the Buddhist concepts of dukkha, karma and the Middle Way and give an informed account of a Buddhist view of happiness
- consider the challenges people face in today's world, reflect on how a Buddhist response – and one other – might bring happiness, and express my personal insights.

This unit helps students in Scotland to achieve RME 3-04a and 3-04b.

Note: The levels used in the Outcomes column have been derived from the 2004 Non-statutory National Framework for RE. These are still found extensively in agreed syllabuses in England, but teachers are advised to consult the statutory requirements applicable to their school, as assessment processes change.

A Buddhist talks about happiness

Is happiness about escaping from dukkha?

No. 'Escaping' implies that one performs an activity that allows one to forget suffering for a short while (e.g. distracting ourselves with TV or X-Box, going on holiday, drinking alcohol or taking drugs, and so on, to escape from the reality that one is experiencing). This route only masks the unhappiness for a short while and often compounds a person's misery.

There are three levels of suffering, as explained by the Buddha:

1. **Ordinary suffering**: that of being born, growing up, growing old, illness and dying.
2. **The suffering of change:** the anxiety or stress someone experiences by trying to hold on to that which always changes.
3. **The suffering of our conditioned state:** a basic dissatisfaction pervading all forms of existence, because all forms of life are changing, impermanent and without any inner core or substance. This includes a sense that nothing ever measures up to our expectation.

As Mahayana Buddhists, right from the start we are taught about The Middle Way. The Middle Way is all about being realistic:

- not allowing painful experiences to make you depressed and not becoming over-excited about seemingly pleasurable experiences
- knowing that all things pass and trying to enjoy life, especially finding enjoyment in the environment, for example by creating a small footprint in the world and finding pleasure in what we see.

The cessation of suffering is peace. When we are at peace then we feel contentment and a gentle happiness. People may harm my body but they cannot touch my mind. They can kill me only once. My mind is my own and travels to my next life. In this way we develop a balanced view of this life which brings happiness.

The state of complete cessation of disturbing attitudes is called liberation – nirvana/nibbana. This is a state of living with equanimity in this very lifetime. The person reaching this stage is called an Arhat. If from then we develop ourselves further and get rid of all of our minor negative habits and develop all of our positive qualities – then we are able to reach Buddhahood.

Venerable Tsuiltrim Tenzin Choesang is a Tibetan Buddhist nun. We asked her a series of questions about Buddhist ideas of happiness.

What actions would lead a Buddhist to happiness?

An understanding of karma, using this understanding to change our lives both mentally and physically. For example, being kind to someone plants a positive seed, which will have a positive result. By looking out for such opportunities, we are changing our minds through thinking and acting. I use the term 'karmic piggy bank' to explain that we work happily to fill our karmic piggy bank with positive thoughts and actions, then we can be sure of something good happening to us in the future. Here are some ways of achieving positive karma:

- by genuinely enjoying the pleasure of others
- by learning to live with less
- by putting others first – with a genuinely positive feeling of care or regard
- by enjoying today fully and not trying to live tomorrow today
- by being realistic about our expectations.

On this page you can find the rest of Venerable Tsuiltrim Tenzin Choesang's interview. Match the responses below to the following questions.

1 Is it fair to say that Buddhism is a search for happiness?

2 What is a Buddhist view of happiness?

3 What attitudes would lead a Buddhist to happiness?

4 How can practices such as meditation lead a Buddhist to happiness?

5 Do people who feel that they are happy experience unhappiness?

A

The Buddha first taught about happiness by describing the current state of most people: a state of unhappiness, or suffering. He then gave explanations and guidelines on how to stop a person's miserable perception of life, all described within the Four Noble Truths.

I think it is helpful to think about the Four Noble Truths in reverse – start by thinking about happiness, how to get to it and what stops us from becoming happy. Happiness is not about purchasing the latest gizmo, make-up, clothing, and so on, or paying to experience a film, food or drugs. Instead, it is an understanding that most of this kind of way of life is a recipe for dukkha. You might use words like anxiety, stress, sadness, discontentment, dissatisfaction, disappointment and disenchantment to get to grips with the idea of dukkha.

By analysing and understanding the root cause of our own personal happiness and unhappiness we can then understand the Buddha's approach. Along the way, a side effect of our practice is that we become more sanguine, more content and hence happier. Whether reaching for Nirvana (Nibbana) or the greater goal of Buddhahood, understanding karma allows us to use the Buddha's guidance to improve our understanding of what makes us truly happy, hence our lifestyle changes accordingly.

B

Yes. A feeling of happiness, even if achieved at the level of Nirvana, does not mean that someone does not recognise negative events in his or her life. However, by holding a firm foundation in understanding karma and the rest of the 'toolkit' towards Buddhahood, a person is basically well grounded and doesn't dwell on the negative aspects of life unduly.

Instead, we remember that all things pass – therefore there is an end to specific happenings that give a feeling of unhappiness as well as happiness. We also gain a firm understanding that we have created the causes for this unhappy incident to occur – so we feel blessed that one more piece of negative karma has ripened. At the end of the day, how we perceive an experience, how we deal with it and how long we hold on to it makes a big difference.

C

- By relaxing in meditation in the morning, we have a calm outlook to the start of the day.
- It helps us control, then reduce our anger.
- It helps us clear our minds so that we do not feel stressed or have a headache.
- It slows our minds down so that we can think things through more calmly.
- It lengthens our lifespan and keeps us looking younger.
- By taking longer, slower breaths we keep fit internally.
- Things that used to make one unhappy no longer have the same effect.
- Happiness is a side effect of all the above and no single action can bring one to a settled state of happiness.

D

- accepting other people's viewpoints
- by turning the 'I' and 'You' into 'We'
- by getting rid of our anger
- by reducing our ego to a level that is just enough for self-preservation in today's Western society
- by loving and/or caring for others for who they are and what they bring to our experience, and not by trying to change anyone to our personal viewpoint and idea of how they should behave
- by not drinking alcohol or taking drugs, not just because they ruin one's health and cost a lot of money, which is wasted, but also because we are not in control of our actions.

E

No. Happiness is the by-product of working towards Nirvana and Buddhahood. Those following the Buddhist way of life fall into two broad groups:

a those following the Theravada route (the way of the Elders), whose goal is to reach Nirvana/Nibbana

b the Mahayana/Vajrayana (Tantrayana) practitioners, whose aim is to reach Buddhahood for the sake of all sentient beings.

Applying a Buddhist approach to happiness

Three levels of suffering
In each box write or draw an example of the type of suffering.

Ordinary suffering

Change suffering

Conditioned state suffering

Middle Way
How might a Buddhist deal with this suffering?

Ordinary suffering

Change suffering

Conditioned state suffering

What's the impact?
Give examples of how this suffering might be felt by a non-Buddhist.

Ordinary suffering

Change suffering

Conditioned state suffering

Recipes for happiness

Ten keys to happier living

Giving: do things for others
Relating: connect with people
Exercising: take care of your body
Appreciating: notice the world around you
Trying out: keep learning new things
Direction: have goals to look forward to
Resilience: find ways to bounce back
Emotion: take a positive approach
Acceptance: be comfortable with who you are
Meaning: be part of something bigger

Action for Happiness
http://www.actionforhappiness.org/10-keys-to-happier-living

How to be happy: advice from Ancient Greece

Don't worry about the gods: they're not interested in you (neither are fate or chance).

Don't worry about death: when we exist, death is not yet present, and when death is present, then we do not exist.

Pleasure is the key to happiness, but we need to think about what will bring us contentment and what will bring anxiety.

Everything we need to be happy is easy to get hold of. You should learn to love the simple life: it's easier to avoid anxiety if you don't get the taste for indulgence.

Epicurus, 341–271 BCE

What makes people happy?

Being with other people

When we can trust people and be trusted

We're not too keen on change

It's better if we don't try to compare our status with others all the time

As we get used to things, the benefits of more stuff soon wears off, so we should not run after having more stuff

Our inner life is as important as our outer circumstances, so we should accept ourselves better and feel more for others.

Adapted from Richard Layard, Happiness: Lessons from a New Science, *Penguin 2005*

A Christian recipe

Be full of joy in the Lord always. I will say again, be full of joy.

Let everyone see that you are gentle and kind. The Lord is coming soon. Do not worry about anything, but pray and ask God for everything you need, always giving thanks. And God's peace, which is so great we cannot understand it, will keep your hearts and minds in Christ Jesus.

Brothers and sisters, think about the things that are good and worthy of praise. Think about the things that are true and honourable and right and pure and beautiful and respected. Do what you learned and received from me, what I told you, and what you saw me do. And the God who gives peace will be with you.

Advice from the Apostle Paul, in his letter to the Philippians, chapter 4, verses 4–9 (NCV)

Topical film: Africa United

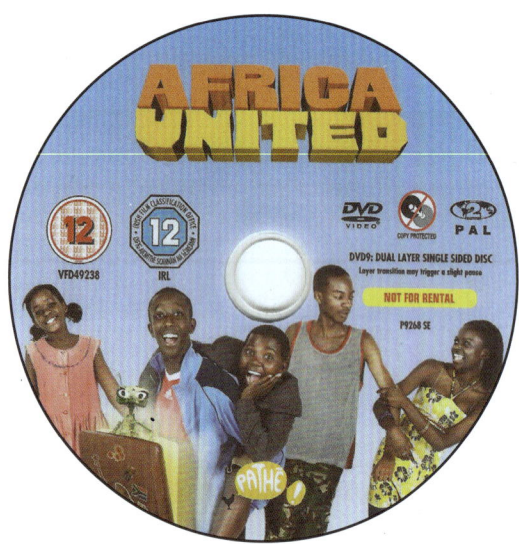

Synopsis

Dudu Kayenzi, a young AIDS orphan from Rwanda, persuades his football-prodigy friend Fabrice to try out for a trial to be part of the opening ceremony for the 2010 World Cup in South Africa. With Dudu's younger sister, Beatrice, the children decide to get a bus to Kigali for the audition. However, through a series of mishaps they end up in Congo instead.

With no papers or money, they are taken to a refugee camp. There they meet Foreman George, a troubled teenager and child soldier who leads them out of the camp to escape the attentions of some of his fellow soldiers. Still pursued, they decide to make their way to Johannesburg in time for the opening ceremony. They cross Lake Tanganyika and meet Celeste, a teenager caught up in the sex trade, working at a smart resort. Celeste joins them in their adventures.

Out of money, Dudu takes them to an AIDS clinic, where cash incentives are offered for having HIV tests. Before long, Dudu falls for a scam as they cross into Zimbabwe, losing all the money. Overnight, Dudu falls ill with tuberculosis (TB) and the others manage to get him to a local mission hospital. Dudu's illness is stabilised but his friends are shocked to discover that he is HIV-positive and vulnerable to the TB, for which the hospital do not have the correct medication. Dudu persuades them they must continue their journey, but Beatrice decides she will stay at the mission hospital, where there is a space for her at the school.

The friends overcome more obstacles to make it to the stadium for the opening ceremony, but Dudu – optimistic to the last – succumbs to his illness and dies.

You might use *Africa United* to explore the following questions:

 **Do you need money to be happy?**

Most people would agree that 'money can't buy you happiness'. A Gallup Poll in 2013 found that some of the poorest countries in the world are the happiest – including Panama, El Salvador and Paraguay. UK interest in our 'wellbeing' claims that, despite significant rises in material prosperity over the last decades, UK happiness has not increased. So, the message is: we must work harder at what makes us happy, not try to make more money!

At first sight, *Africa United* might support this view. After all, despite the poverty, illness, threat and danger that they face, Dudu and his friends often show signs that they are happy. Perhaps Dudu appears happier than Fabrice's relatively wealthy mother. But clearly the need for basic material goods are essential for survival – and it is rather patronising to suggest that people should make do with being 'poor but happy'. It is an easy view to take from our comparatively (excessively?) wealthy viewpoint, with our easy access to clean water, food, healthcare and education.

But, accepting that it would be better for Dudu and his friends to have these fundamental needs met, what is it that makes them happy? Are there things that are more important than material wellbeing?

Students might identify the group's friendship and mutual support in the face of challenges, their desire to make it to the end of their journey, and, for Beatrice, perhaps her clear and straightforward trust in God and the power of prayer. How far do any of these contribute to students' own happiness?

 **How much is happiness dependent upon circumstances or upon your personality?**

Dudu is clearly a boy of irrepressible energy and enthusiasm. Despite being HIV-positive, his zest for life is inspiring. Is that down to his personality, or is it possible for people to rise above their circumstances?

Research[1] claims that only 10 per cent of our happiness is dependent upon our circumstances (income, education, neighbourhood and so forth); 50 per cent is dependent upon our 'set point', our general temperament, a combination of nature and nurture. However, this leaves 40 per cent of our happiness as a result of our 'intentional activities' – our motivations, things we choose to do and ways we choose to think. This is why organisations like Action for Happiness encourage a series of '10 keys to happier living'.[2]

While they await the HIV testing, each character responds differently. Celeste is afraid of the possible bad news. This fear of the unknown seems to be more debilitating than for Dudu, who does know that he is HIV-positive. Many therapies try to help people develop less fearful responses to what might happen – a way of changing our 'intentional activities'.

This book explores some of the ways in which religions encourage believers to direct their 'intentional activities' – students might explore the extent to which these lead to religious believers being happier than others.

 Do you have to *feel* happy all the time to *be* happy?

The film is an optimistic presentation of what is in reality a dark and difficult life – these children have to face bereavement, illness, poverty, lack of education, violence and death. Most of our students thankfully do not generally face these kinds of pressures, but life is not all pleasure and happy emotions. Is it possible to *be* happy overall – to see through the times when you *feel* unhappy, the times of difficulty? This would require an understanding of happiness that is not just about feelings, of course. Perhaps a wider view of happiness in terms of overall life satisfaction allows us to handle difficult times.

 How far does having a goal in life affect our happiness?

The decision to travel so that Fabrice can show his skills at the World Cup ceremony drives Dudu and his friends. They are caught up in this dream, and this gives them the motivation to keep going in the face of danger and setback. The excitement of the final attendance makes their trials seem worthwhile, and to offer a tribute to the memory of Dudu's joyous spirit and energy. Beatrice's goal of finding a cure for AIDS gives her the courage to leave her friends and seek an education at the mission hospital.

Evidence suggests that having an overall purpose for life can affect a person's sense of happiness. This means that they maintain their equanimity in the face of difficulties, as they have a more important goal that transcends moment-to-moment feelings or more significant setbacks. It is plausible to suggest that this is one reason why people of religious faith routinely poll higher in terms of self-reported happiness than people with no religious faith. Most religions teach that there is some ultimate meaning and purpose to life, as well as offering a person the resources to cope with the exigencies of life. Their description of life's meaning and purpose might be wrong, of course, and religious believers do not necessarily handle challenges better than anyone else, but how might people find benefit in the hope that religions offer?

 Some texts to think about:

Jesus said: 'Therefore I tell you, do not worry about your life, what you will eat or drink; or about your body, what you will wear. Is not life more than food, and the body more than clothes? … Can any one of you by worrying add a single hour to your life? … But seek first [your heavenly Father's] kingdom and his righteousness, and all these things will be given to you as well. Therefore do not worry about tomorrow, for tomorrow will worry about itself. Each day has enough trouble of its own.'

Matthew 6: 25–27, 33–34 [NIV]

We do not lose heart… For our light and momentary troubles are achieving for us an eternal glory that far outweighs them all. So we fix our eyes not on what is seen, but on what is unseen, since what is seen is temporary, but what is unseen is eternal.

2 Corinthians 4:16–18 [NIV]

All those who are unhappy in this world are so because they desire only their own happiness. All those who are happy in this world are so because they desire only the happiness of others.

Santideva, Bodhicaryavatara, Bk 3

 Resources

1. K M Sheldon and S Lyubomirsky, 'Achieving sustainable new happiness: prospects, practices, and prescriptions' in A Linley and S Joseph (eds) *Positive Psychology in Practice* (Hoboken, NJ: John Wiley & Sons 2004), pp.127–45.
2. http://www.actionforhappiness.org/10-keys-to-happier-living. See also p.15 in this volume.

What do we do when unhappiness comes? Exploring the Book of Job

Overview

Happiness is almost universally desired, but none of us enjoys only happiness in life. Resilience in the face of trouble is a virtue admired in all religions, and – rather recently – in many schools. This unit of work offers a way of studying ancient wisdom that opens up questions about God, faith and life's tragedies through narrative.

The work has an investigative, problem-centred character: teachers will facilitate this learning, but not often lead it. The aim is for students to articulate their own ideas with increasing depth and clarity, supporting their viewpoints with reasons and arguments.

Essential knowledge

The 'problem of suffering' stems from the fact that humans experience and observe suffering that may be profoundly painful and enduringly damaging in life. This fact seems to count against the existence of a great God full of love, the maker of all and the lover of each. Would such a God not help us?

For believers in one God (including, of course, Jews and Christians as well as Muslims, Sikhs and Bahá'ís), the questions raised by suffering or unhappiness might be reframed. They might be less concerned with the existence of God, or even God's nature, and more about God's presence and purpose: Where is God when unhappiness comes? How can faith be maintained in unhappy times? Does God allow unhappiness for any kind of purpose?

The biblical book of Job offers a narrative response of real profundity to the issue 'How do humans respond when unhappiness comes?' Job is a good man who loses everything in a catastrophic series of events. He refuses to reject God but he does get angry and rail at God, asking for an explanation of why he is going through all this. Some of his friends support him in his suffering, but he rejects their explanations: he cannot accept that he deserves his lot. Eventually, after demanding that God answers his questions, the climax of the narrative comes with a direct encounter between Job and God. God offers no explanation except to remind Job of who he is. It seems to satisfy Job, who appears to have learned much through his experiences. However, this raises fresh questions: does the experience of God's presence through suffering dissolve (rather than solve) the problem in some way? If so, how?

Essential teaching and learning

This unit asks students to think about religious and atheist responses to unhappiness and suffering in life. They will develop their skills in interpretation from a study of the biblical book of Job, in which an innocent person's happiness is destroyed by disasters, leading to profound questioning of God: why does he not do something? Is he responsible for Job's sufferings? Is he responsible for sufferings today?

In modern terms, the narrative also explores the 'argument for God from religious experience': if a suffering person senses God's absence or presence, does that make a difference? The book of Job is not really a philosophical response to a rational problem: it is a visceral engagement with what it means to be human as well.

13–16

Context

This unit connects well with work on questions of meaning and purpose in RE for both 11–14s and 14–19s. The work connects most closely to Judaism and Christianity, where the book of Job is scripture. In Islam, Prophet Ayyub (Job) is a key figure too.

You could also use this in relation to learning about the problem of suffering at GCSE or Standard Grade.

Resources/links

 For NATRE members and *REtoday* subscribers, Lat Blaylock has recorded a short retelling of the story of Job, using the artwork of Si Smith, which you can show to students, available via our website www.retoday.org.uk.

Further resources, aimed at older students, can be found in dare2engage's *Rage, Despair, Hope* DVD and postcards, available from RE Today Services.

BBC's recent RE 14–19 series *A Question of Faith* includes a programme on suffering in which an atheist, Muslim and Christian visit a children's hospice and explore the issues arising. See: www.bbc.co.uk/programmes/p01w6tw7

Well-known theologian and philosopher William Lane Craig blogs on the problem of evil, and engages with the issues in depth. Find related resources here to explore Job further. www.bethinking.org/suffering/the-problem-of-evil

Learning activities

1 Speculate: raising questions and developing initial responses

Begin by giving students in pairs or threes the picture page (p.20), and ask them to stick it onto a larger piece of paper and consider what story the pictures might tell. Get them to write some questions about the pictures around the edge (leave some space for Activity 2). Use the usual enquiry prompts: who/what/which/where/when/why/what if ...? Pass their paper to another pair. Tell the students that the seven pictures are part of a modern artist's response to the book of Job. The book explores ideas of unhappiness, God and human suffering. In his suffering, Job accuses God of picking on him. Does this information help them to answer any of their questions? What indication do Job's words (including some vivid imagery) give of Job's view of, and feelings towards, God?

2 Working with the story of Job

Give the students a set of eight text cards, cut out from a copy of p.21: one is a title card; the others tell the story of Job and use some of the imagery, poetry and questions of the book to raise more questions. Ask students to match the cards to the seven pictures, stick them around the images from Activity 1, draw lines to link them and write the reason for the link along the line. Can they sequence the text cards? The story runs down the columns. (NATRE members can use the short retelling of Job online: see p.18). Can they now answer some of the questions raised in Activity 1? Can they add four more questions, not about the story, but questions for God about unhappiness? Why do they think Job responded to God like this at the end? Look up the final chapter of the story in Job 42. Was it all worth it?

3 Exploring responses to unhappiness in the light of the Job story

On p.22 there are three viewpoints, one Jewish, one Christian and one atheist, on suffering, God and unhappiness. Give students a copy of the page, and invite them to read these aloud, highlight the sentences they agree/disagree with in each one, and discuss the questions raised. What is surprising about these responses?

4 Ranking nine responses

Next give the students a copy of p.23. This resource extends their learning by giving some contemporary responses to unhappiness. They might cut up the worksheet and organise the responses in a 1–9 ranking, or a Diamond 9 ranking. The task sheet gives them some ways of writing about their own ideas.

5 Dear Job ...

Ask students to devise some 'agony aunt' letters from religious believers today to write to Job. How might Job reply? From what they have learned about him, how would he respond? He probably wouldn't give easy answers. What would their own replies be? Whose is best?

6 A booklet of reasons and arguments: a possible creative addition

Ask students to create a booklet of ideas for responding to unhappiness and suffering. They might use several of the Job images as starting points, and then reflect on how people with and without religious beliefs might respond. If belief in God can comfort some, from where might agnostics and atheists gain comfort? Suggest they might bring together learning from previous RE studies and include wise advice, song lyrics, quotations and (most importantly) their own ideas.

Outcomes

Students can demonstrate achievement at levels 4–6 in these activities if they can say 'yes' to some of these 'I can' statements.

Description of achievement

I can ...

Level 4

- show that I understand how the story of Job pictures a religious person reacting to suffering

- ask good questions about God, suffering and unhappiness prompted by the Bible book of Job.

Level 5

- explain ways the sense of the presence of God has an impact for believers when they suffer

- suggest varied answers to questions raised by considering religious responses to suffering.

Level 6

- interpret the biblical narrative of Job in relation to questions about suffering, meaning and purpose, giving insights of my own

- argue insightfully and reasonably for my own account of why and how people continue to believe in God despite suffering and pain.

This unit helps students in Scotland to achieve RME 4-01a

Note: The levels used in the Outcomes column have been derived from the 2004 *Non-statutory National Framework for RE*. These are still found extensively in agreed syllabuses in England, but teachers are advised to consult the statutory requirements applicable to their school, as assessment processes change.

Seven images from the Job narrative

© Si Smith

When unhappiness comes

The Story of Job
Ancient wisdom?
Getting angry with God?

There was a man who lived long ago, out East, who was blessed in every way. He had 5000 camels, 3000 cattle, 500 donkeys. He had three daughters and seven sons.

He always praised God for all the good things he received and his life was admired by all who knew him. His name was Job.

Then guess what happened?

One day came Satan the Evil One to God's court, saying: 'Well, he only praises you for all you give him. Take his stuff, and he'll curse you to your face.'
Then God said 'Try. But I think not.'
In one day there came thieves, and raiders, robbers and plunderers who stole or killed all Job's cattle, flocks and herds.
That same day came a whirlwind upon the house where all his children partied, to flatten it and kill them all.
Job was devastated.

'Naked I came to birth,
Naked I will return to Earth.
God gave, and God takes,'
said Job, never cursing his maker.
But in deep sorrow he asked his friends [and God as well] hard questions:
'Why can't the day of my birth be blotted out?
Why must we suffer the time of our lives in pain?
What's the point? What is God playing at?
Why must I endure this utter unhappiness?'

While sores erupted over all his body, and his friends made irritating comments blaming him for his pains, Job was broken to the point of despair by his loss.
'I am surrounded by dogs!
Jackals wait to eat my dead flesh!
My body is corrupted by sickness!
God, what are you doing?
Why don't you put in an appearance?
I'd like to drag you to court!
You're supposed to help us!'

'God, they say you're so high and mighty.
Everyone is supposed to bow and be silent.
I won't be silent!
You (yes, you) are the one who hurts me.
You've failed to be my protector.
You're supposed to be my defender
but it's you who attacks me,
you who leaves me suffering.
You crush me like a bug, God.
My woe is all your fault.'

'Humans think it's hard to mine diamonds,
Tunnelling deep into the core of the earth.
That's easy compared to working out what God is doing.
Diamonds are cheap compared to knowing your plan, O "God of Love".
Where are you when it hurts down here on Earth, you "Mighty One"?
Are you hiding?
It's time you showed up to defend yourself.
Come on. Speak!'

Then God did speak to Job, out of a whirlwind:
'Job, you ask so much, but you know too little. You ask so many questions; let me ask you some. Where were you when I spun the stars into space? What do you know of the ages of time and the acres of eternity? Can you walk the star fields and see the end from the beginning?'
Then Job was very moved. 'Up till now, people told me about you, but now I've seen you with my own eyes,' he said. 'I am sorry. I am satisfied.'

Responses to suffering: three voices

" I'm David, and I'm Jewish. Most people know what the Nazis tried to do to the Jews – there is a source of unhappiness much worse even than poor old Job. The Holocaust led some Jews to stop believing G–d is good and great. But Job never did that: he wanted God to speak. Most Jews also continue to have faith. My own way of looking at it is that God's knowledge and goodness compares to mine like a giant to an ant: from human perspectives we see so little (which is what Job notices at the end). Sometimes people find goodness through suffering, sometimes rescue comes after despair. Sometimes it doesn't. But the Almighty has made this world, with both beauty and sorrow in it. I choose still to trust in G–d, despite the sufferings that have come upon Jewish people. In that sense, I am with Job as he feels at the end of his story. "

" I'm Jackie, and I'm an atheist. It is puzzling to me that people go on believing in this so-called 'God of love'. It is rather obvious to me that if God was real, then the suffering and unhappiness of things like HIV, cancer, tsunamis and earthquakes would not happen. Job's story of tragic events doesn't surprise me: these things happen because we are fragile humans on a planet of titanic forces. What surprises me is that god-believers carry on with what I think is a superstitious idea. Some believers say this is some kind of test from God, but that implies a god who is an experimenter on humans – not very loving. I think we need to accept that the world is rather random, including good and bad. Life just does involve suffering and sadness and, when it comes, we don't try to explain it but comfort each other, work hard against it, take advice. I sometimes try to ignore it! Best to live your life as well as you can, avoiding the worst and making the most of the good bits. Max the happy and min the sad. "

" I'm Sam. I'm a Christian. I love the story of Job because it shows there isn't really an argument that will tell us why we suffer. Instead, Job has a kind of spiritual experience. He gets really angry about suffering, of course – who wouldn't? Tragedies hit him like a hammer one after the other. I like the way the story shows that friends who will stick with you may get shouted at, but at least they hang in there. Then at the end when God speaks out of the whirlwind, I think Job feels sorry for some of what he says – he uses bad language to God, and he perhaps feels kind of overwhelmed as well. Christians believe that God suffers with us – that's what the story of Jesus on the cross shows. God's love involves entering into our pains, and walking beside us as we suffer. Sometimes I feel that God is absent and has abandoned me, but often I find that God can be with me in sad times. His presence is really important to me.

What do you do when unhappiness comes? Rank nine responses

Here are nine responses to unhappiness. Which ones do you think are closest to Job's responses? What do you think of these responses? Which ones are close to your own responses? Are there any responses from which you could learn, or that you might try out when you are unhappy? Read these aloud carefully with a partner, and weigh them up: which ones make sense to you?

Unhappiness leads to rage and fury. This may not solve much, but it is natural, and it can be helpful to blow your top and rage against the machine. Let it out!	**In my spiritual life I use contemplation, sitting still and focusing on an image of Christ and some words from the gospel. For me, this is a great way to achieve calmness when I'm unhappy.**	**Unhappiness can be good, in a weird way: when I am unhappy, I try to look for the reasons why, and see if I can change my life and live more at ease with myself.**
In the Jewish Bible, a poet says to himself: 'Why are you downcast, my soul? Why are you anxious inside me? Hope in God. You will praise him again.' I try to be patient with my unhappiness.	**Occasionally in my life, at times of deepest distress, I've felt a strange and unexplainable sense of the presence of God. You can't force this, but it is priceless. I think Job felt it too.**	**The main thing that helps me with unhappiness is distraction. I play on the X-Box, or go out with friends, have a few drinks, and try to drown my sorrows. It usually works (till the next morning).**
When I'm unhappy, I pray for peace in my heart and the ability to change my situation. I ask God for help.	**Unhappiness can attack you through circumstances: you lose someone, you don't get what you want. But it's how we respond that matters: I fight back with positivity.**	**Come out fighting. Take no rubbish. Don't let them grind you down. Stick it to the Man.**

Questions for discussion and written work

- Take time to reflect on your responses to unhappiness. Which of the nine above are close to yours? Why?
- Religions offer their followers roads to happiness, in many ways. Four of the nine ideas above deal with this. Which ones do you disagree with most, and why?
- What would your advice be for dealing with unhappiness? Discuss your ideas, then write your five-point plan, offering guidance for teenagers when unhappiness strikes.

Is happiness the same as pleasure? Applying ethical hedonism

Overview

This unit explores the ethical thinking behind the idea of *hedonism*. Students will consider the work of Jeremy Bentham, the influential eighteenth-century ethical hedonist. Students will assess his 'Hedonic Calculus' – his attempt to calculate whether an action is morally good or bad depending on the amount of pleasure it yields.

Finally, students will compare Bentham's ethical hedonism to virtue ethics in order to evaluate the Hedonic Calculus and discuss whether happiness and pleasure are the same thing.

Essential knowledge

Jeremy Bentham (1748–1832) argued that happiness is no more or less than physical comfort and the absence of pain. This is the stance of an ethical hedonist, from the Greek *hedone*, meaning 'pleasure'. For Bentham and other hedonists, to increase the sum of pleasure in the world is a moral act. Bentham's theory of Utilitarianism and John Stuart Mill's development of this ethical model are appropriate for study post-16. However, in this set of activities, the focus is on the view of happiness offered by ethical hedonism.

A more holistic view of happiness is found in virtue ethics, which students will compare to ethical hedonism. Virtue theory, as espoused by Aristotle in the fourth century BCE, is not about following a set of calculations, but living in a habitually virtuous way. According to Aristotle, all people are searching for *eudaimonia*, variously translated as the 'greatest good', 'supreme happiness' or 'human flourishing'. This is a state of spiritual and physical blessedness for oneself and one's community. In endeavouring to attain this state we practise virtuous living daily, not by following rules but by inhabiting a total ethical outlook.

Both these visions of happiness, pleasure and satisfaction enable students to weigh up whether happiness is indeed simply freedom from pain and having one's physical needs met, or something more spiritual and communal.

Essential teaching and learning

The key learning here is a significant ethical position, which has religious as well as philosophical implications. The first three tasks give students time and space to grasp the concept of hedonism in enough depth to evaluate it.

The process of applying an ethical theory to contemporary dilemmas is offered both for understanding the theory and general development. If students find this process difficult and have lots of questions, be open to what they find hard and allow time for discussion about both the process itself and the *value* of the process. Students might love it or hate it, but they will have learned something valuable about ethics! Less time is given to virtue ethics as here it serves as a comparison to ethical hedonism, but it is a significant ethical position in its own right and it would be appropriate to explore it in more depth, if time allows.

Students should be able to critique both ethical outlooks and articulate their own view of the relationship between happiness and pleasure at the end of this unit.

14–16

Context

This unit can offer a non-religious ethical view for use in RS GCSE and Standard Grade examination work, applying Bentham's Hedonic Calculus to the ethical situations they are likely to encounter in an exam syllabus. Moreover, learning these key ethical theories is a good taster for those thinking of taking RS further.

Resources/links

Clear and concise BBC page on consequentialist ethics, including Utilitarianism: http://www.bbc.co.uk/ethics/introduction/consequentialism_1.shtml

Comparison BBC page on virtue ethics: http://www.bbc.co.uk/ethics/introduction/virtue.shtml

Peter Singer's contribution to *Jewcy* http://jewcy.com/post/petersingerjewcy

Peter Singer's Princeton webpage. Click on 'how to make a difference' to find out about his charitable work: https://www.princeton.edu/~psinger/

Learning activities

1 Is the search for pleasure a moral good?

a Supply plenty of magazines and ask students to create a collage using images of what makes them happy. Display around the room. Allow time to peruse.

b As a class, categorise all the things that make people happy: how many, broadly, are about 'pleasure' and how many are about 'happiness'? Discuss the differences.

c Display this statement: 'Nature has placed mankind under the governance of two sovereign masters, pain and pleasure.' (Jeremy Bentham, *Principles of Morals and Legislation*, 1789, Chapter 1, 1). Teach about Bentham's theory of *ethical hedonism*: the view that all human beings are motivated by the search for pleasure and the avoidance of pain. For Bentham, pleasure was morally good and pain was morally bad. Do students agree or disagree with this view? Can seeking pleasure be a moral end? Do they have examples in their collages?

2 Can pleasure be measured?

a Bring junk materials in and ask groups of students to create a 'hedonism machine' – a contraption to measure how much pleasure an act or situation creates. Students explain their machines. Teenage boys might immediately think about sex, perhaps … so you could avoid this entirely, or take the chance to talk about whether physical pleasure is the only kind.

b Explain to the class that Bentham set out to do just this: design a method of determining how much pleasure or pain an action or situation causes. Bentham's guiding principle was to achieve *the greatest happiness for the greatest number of people*. In order to decide how to achieve this, he created the **Hedonic Calculus**.

c Hand out p.26. Read the seven factors in the Hedonic Calculus and get students to complete the table.

d Compare to their own hedonic-calculation machines. Had they broken down pleasure in this much detail? Were they working to similar lines?

e Read the quotations on p.26. Do students find any that persuade them that pleasure is a moral good? Is it right, or selfish, or meaningless, for example?

3 Applying the Hedonic Calculus

a Copy and hand out pp.28–29, which ask students to apply the Hedonic Calculus to four moral dilemmas. Do this in pairs or groups. You may not wish all students to attempt every dilemma.

b The aim is to evaluate the Hedonic Calculus when applied to real situations. Be open to the questions and problems raised as students engage in the process. Record these questions for the ensuing discussion.

c Discuss: Can pleasure can be calculated in this mechanistic way? Is pleasure the same thing as happiness?

4 Compared to virtue ethics

a Introduce the idea of virtue ethics: an ethical outlook developed not from calculating the amount of pleasure associated with a particular situation, but from cultivating a virtuous character, whatever the situation. Define 'virtue'.

b Copy and hand out p.27. Ask the class to suggest all the virtues they can think of which are needed in the twenty-first century (e.g. justice, courage, love, charity). Ask each group or pair to choose the three most important and record on p.27.

c Ask pairs or groups to return to the four ethical dilemmas and record what the response would be when applying virtue ethics. There is space for students to enter their own views on the dilemmas. Share these analyses.

d Discuss which 'greatest good' students would be more inclined to aim for and why: Aristotle's or Bentham's.

Outcomes

Students can demonstrate achievement at levels 5–8 if they can say 'yes' to some of these 'I can' statements.

Description of achievement

I can …

Level 5

- give an accurate account of ethical hedonism

- explain the purpose of the Hedonic Calculus.

Level 6

- explain *why* Bentham equated pleasure with the moral good

- give a reasoned argument for or against ethical hedonism.

Level 7

- articulate, with reference to ethical hedonism and virtue ethics, a view of happiness

- evaluate the vision of happiness found within either ethical hedonism or virtue ethics, expressing their own insights.

Level 8

- offer a reasoned response to the value of centuries-old ethical principles today

- evaluate critically and personally either ethical hedonism or virtue ethics with reference to the needs of our twenty-first-century world.

This unit helps students in Scotland to achieve RME 4-02b.

Note: The levels used in the Outcomes column have been derived from the 2004 *Non-statutory National Framework for RE*. These are still found extensively in agreed syllabuses in England, but teachers are advised to consult the statutory requirements applicable to their school, as assessment processes change.

Calculating pleasure and pain

Bentham sought to maximise pleasure and minimise pain for the most people possible.

His Hedonic Calculus is a method for determining how much pleasure an action or situation will cause, as well as the quality of the pleasure.

> When considering how much pleasure results from an action, you must consider…
> 1 Its intensity
> 2 Its duration
> 3 Its certainty or uncertainty
> 4 Its propinquity or remoteness
> 5 Its fecundity
> 6 Its purity
> 7 Its extent
>
> J Bentham *Principles of Morals and Legislation (1789)*

Complete the following table, choosing explanations from the boxes below.

Intensity	
Duration	
Certainty/ uncertainty	
Propinquity/ remoteness	
Fecundity	
Purity	
Extent	

- How long will the pleasure last?
- How soon will the pleasure occur?
- Will it lead to further pleasure?
- Is this pleasure likely to lead to pain at some point afterwards?
- How likely is the pleasure to occur?
- How strong is the pleasure?
- How many people will be affected by the pleasure?

Read these quotations. Do any persuade you that seeking pleasure is a moral end?

I commend the enjoyment of life, because there is nothing better for a person under the sun than to eat and drink and be glad. Then joy will accompany them in their toil all the days of the life God has given them.

Ecclesiastes 8:15 (NIVUK)

Without friends no one would choose to live, though he had all other goods.

Aristotle, Nicomachean Ethics, *Book VIII, 1155.a5*

You can live to be a hundred if you give up all the things that make you want to live to be a hundred.

Woody Allen

The only way to get rid of temptation is to yield to it. Resist it, and your soul grows sick with longing for the things it has forbidden to itself.

Oscar Wilde, The Picture of Dorian Gray

Happiness: pleasure or virtue?

What are the twenty-first century virtues?

1

2

3

Giving to charity	**Fairtrade cotton**
Acceptable in virtue theory? Acceptable in ethical hedonism?	Acceptable in virtue theory? Acceptable in ethical hedonism?
Your view:	Your view:
Abortion Acceptable in virtue theory? Acceptable in ethical hedonism?	**Killing in war** Acceptable in virtue theory? Acceptable in ethical hedonism?
Your view:	Your view:

Which 'greatest good' would you aim for: Aristotle's or Bentham's? Why?

How much happiness? Four dilemmas

Dilemma: Giving to charity

Anyone who has been attacked by charity muggers, or 'chuggers', in the street, or has quickly turned the page in a magazine to avoid a picture of a starving child in a charity advert, has experienced this dilemma. What should we do with our money?

It's your money, why shouldn't you spend it on yourself? Most of what people spend their money on is essential: food, bills, travel, and so on.

The modern Utilitarian thinker Peter Singer argues however that, 'If you are living comfortably while others are hungry or dying from easily preventable diseases, and you are doing nothing about it, there is something wrong with your behaviour.' (Peter Singer: www.jewcy.com/post/petersingerjewcy, May 2007)

Dilemma: Fairtrade cotton

We see images in newspapers of the effects of cheap cotton and cheap labour around the world: children robbed of their education and childhood, working in dangerous sweatshops for a pittance; the wide-scale draining of rivers and inland seas to service cotton factories. But when we walk into a fashionable shop and see a great outfit to wear to tonight's party, we somehow forget our feelings of sympathy for these children and the planet.

Fairtrade cotton represents better opportunities for workers and less environmental destruction, but it is more expensive and less stylish.

Should we be compelled to buy only Fairtrade cotton clothes?

Giving to charity

Who suffers?

Who benefits?

Benefits defined as 'pleasure':

Intensity:

Duration:

Certainty:

Propinquity:

Fecundity:

Purity:

Extent:

Conclusion: can giving to charity lead to the greatest happiness for the greatest number?

Fairtrade cotton

Who suffers?

Who benefits?

Benefits defined as 'pleasure':

Intensity:

Duration:

Certainty:

Propinquity:

Fecundity:

Purity:

Extent:

Conclusion: can buying Fairtrade cotton products lead to the greatest happiness for the greatest number?

Dilemma: Abortion

Abortion prevents the life of (or kills, some would say) a potential human being, yet it is legal and is seen by many as a powerful right to give women the autonomy they are so often denied.

As soon as a baby is born it is a source of joy for parents and the community. How can terminating the life of an innocent, defenceless future person be morally acceptable?

Yet who would wish a child into a life where it was unwanted and unloved, or would be born seriously disabled? Removing a collection of cells from a woman's body long before they are aware can be seen as a loving measure to protect the potential child from a life of suffering.

Dilemma: Killing in war

Can killing in war ever be acceptable? In peacetime it would be seen as murder, the worst crime a human can commit.

Is it noble to put your life on the line to protect your country, even if it makes you into a killer?

Is killing in self-defence or to protect others morally distinct from murder?

Are the generals who give the orders and make a career out of war more responsible for people's lives than the ordinary soldiers who actually engage in fighting?

Abortion

Who suffers?

Who benefits?

Benefits defined as 'pleasure':

Intensity:

Duration:

Certainty:

Propinquity:

Fecundity:

Purity:

Extent:

Conclusion: can abortion lead to the greatest happiness for the greatest number?

Killing in war

Who suffers?

Who benefits?

Benefits defined as 'pleasure':

Intensity:

Duration:

Certainty:

Propinquity:

Fecundity:

Purity:

Extent:

Conclusion: can killing in war lead to the greatest happiness for the greatest number?

Topical
artefact: Happiness jars

A popular way of promoting happiness is through developing gratitude. Here is an image of a 'Happiness Jar' (see http://www.wikihow.com/Keep-a-Happiness-Jar) and from the 'Happijar' app (http://www.happijar.com/).

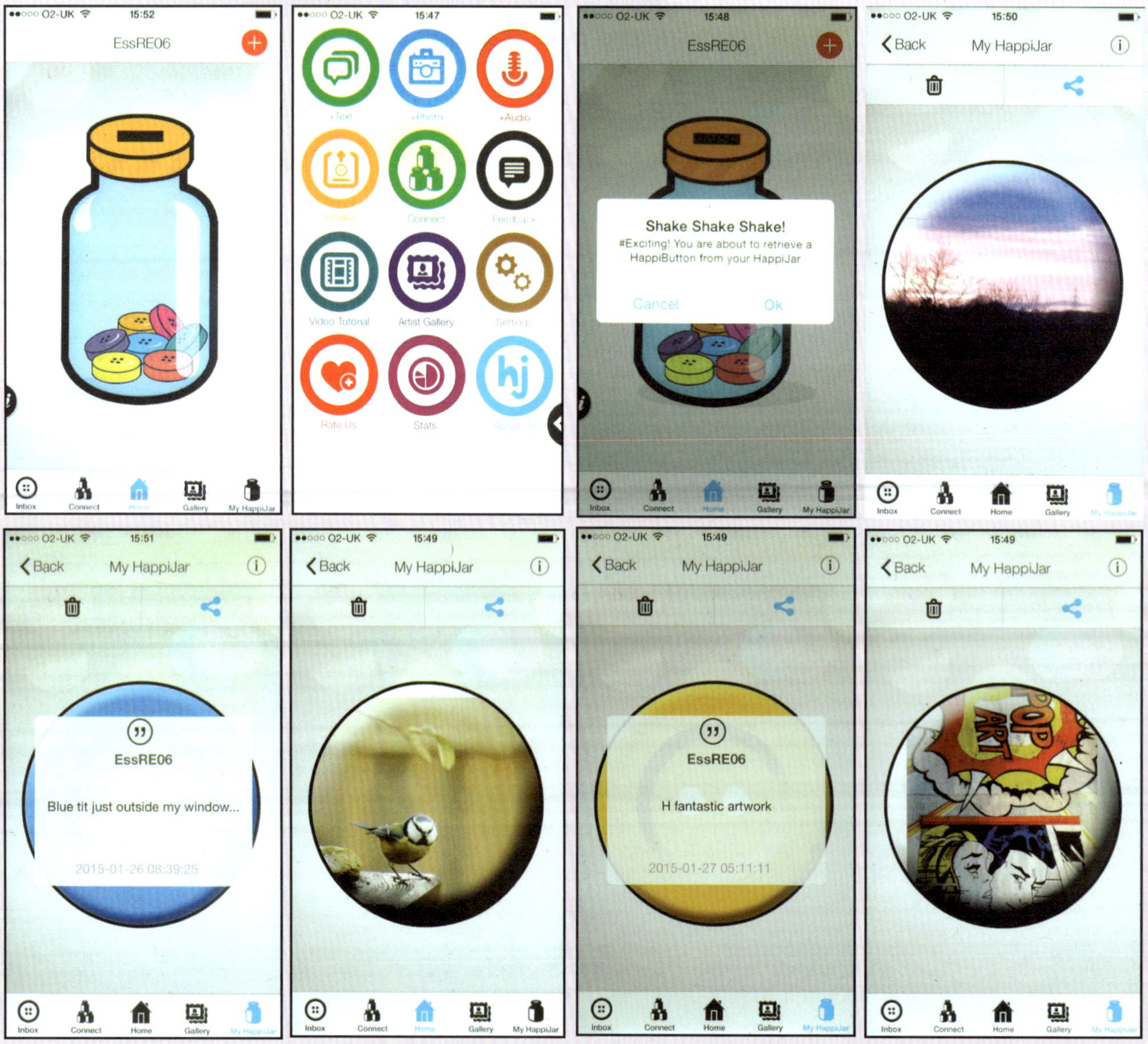

Learning activities

As well as the 'happiness jars' and their 'HappiJar' equivalent from p.30, you can download numerous 'gratitude journals' to help you keep track of the good things that happen to you during the day. Such behaviour, it is argued, leads to happiness.

The rationale involves a kind of cognitive behaviour (self-) therapy, whereby you practise patterns of appreciating what is good in your life, rather than dwelling on what is not good. Gratitude pushes out envy, resentment, disappointment and bitterness, making way for happier states of mind. Some of the app-advocates talk about 'rewiring your brain' in 21 or 30 or 100 days …

Some questions to get you thinking:
- To what extent are we what we think?
- Do good things or bad things have more of an impact on your mind?
- Our brains are flexible – we make new neural connections all the time, and practising something strengthens those connections. So, if it is possible to 'rewire' the brain, why would it be good to focus on gratitude?
- What is the difference between being grateful for good things, and being grateful to a beneficent deity for good things?
- If someone believes that they exist because of a Creator, for what might they be thankful?
- Is it plausible that someone could be thankful in all circumstances? What does it mean? Is this only possible for theists rather than atheists? Is it only possible for optimists rather than realists or pessimists …?
- If you focus on saying 'thank you' because you know it will make you happy, will it make you happy?

Activities

Find out about some of the Jewish blessings, which commonly start 'Baruch atah Adonai' – 'You are blessed, O Lord our God, king of the universe who …' The Talmud advises saying 100 blessings a day. See if your class can think of 100 things to say 'thank you' for. Perhaps your class might have a 'happiness jar' or display. Perhaps your students might try a 'gratitude journal' for a week or two – two or three things to be grateful for every day. Make a point of saying thank you to people, too. See what happens.

Explore what the apostle Paul was saying about being thankful in all circumstances. Read the catalogue of trials Paul faced in 2 Corinthians 11:23–27. Get students to offer ideas about how he could still be thankful in those circumstances. (They may refer to 2 Corinthians 4:16–18 for one idea.) Can students come up with any examples of people who have found something good even in the worst situations?

Compare the idea of a 'happiness jar' and 'gratitude journal' with a prayer journal, or a Tibetan Buddhist prayer flag. What are the similarities and differences? Which might bring more happiness and why, for the individual, their community, or for the world?

Some texts to consider:

Praise the LORD.
Give thanks to the LORD, for he is good;
his love endures for ever.
Psalm 106:1 (NIVUK)

Rejoice always, pray continually; give thanks in all circumstances; for this is God's will for you in Christ Jesus.
1 Thessalonians 5:16–18 (NIVUK)

All that we are is the result of our mind; it is founded on the results of our actions and experiences; our life is the creation of our mind. If a person speaks or acts with an impure mind, pain follows that person, as the wheel follows the foot of the ox that draws the carriage.
If a person speaks or acts with a peaceful mind, happiness follows that person, like a never-departing shadow.
Dhammapada 1–2

Now my dream is to have everyone on the planet addicted to gratitude and on a daily gratitude habit. … If you are truly thankful from the moment you wake up to the moment you go to sleep at night, I promise that you will … harness everything great that life has to offer.
Carla White, getgratitude.co

If you simply try to show appreciation because studies show it makes you feel better, you might actually distort and transform what was good about thankfulness in the first place.
Julian Baggini http://on.ft.com/1Dd9XMH

The ungrateful, envious complaining man … cripples himself. He is focused on what he has not, particularly on that which somebody else has or seems to have, and by that he tends to poison his world.
BV Schwarz, The Human Person and the World of Values, 1971

Years ago I had a Buddhist teacher in Thailand who would remind all his students that there was always something to be thankful for. He'd say, 'Let's rise and be thankful, for if we didn't learn a lot today, at least we may have learned a little. And if we didn't learn even a little, at least we didn't get sick. And if we did get sick, at least we didn't die. So let us all be thankful.'
Leo Buscaglia, Born for Love: Reflections on Loving, 1992

Entry-level activities

Eight sentences for a happy world: the Beatitudes of Jesus

Many religions encourage the pursuit of justice, peace, pure-heartedness and mercy. In Christian scripture, Jesus begins his life as a rabbi with the 'Sermon on the Mount'. At the very beginning of his work, he teaches his followers 'Eight Sentences to Change the World'. These sentences proclaim eight blessings on people who seek to live their lives in particular ways. It is fair to say that they are widely recognised as a piece of spiritual genius. The Beatitudes are not simple, and this entry-level activity will not plumb their depths. See the work as a simple introduction to some 'deep stuff'.

a Ask students to reflect on times when they have been happy. They might write a few sentences or draw some pictures or symbols to show these. Talk about what kinds of experiences bring happiness.

b What do they think makes people happy, most of all? Ask students to complete the sentence, 'You are happy if …' They should complete it in original, detailed and deep ways, and share the results. Students can do two or three each if they like, but 'deep' matters more than 'quick' here.

c Ask students if they would like to see Jesus' answer to this activity. Tell them it is hard to understand in some ways, so we have a 'main version' and a simple version. Give groups of three or four the Bible text of Matthew 5:1–10 in the centre of a sheet of paper and ask the groups to annotate it around the edges with questions about the meaning and ideas of what Jesus said. Then swap papers. Ask the groups to read the simplified version, and see if they can suggest answers to the questions the first group have raised.

d In whole class discussion, consider any parts of the text where the meaning is not clear.

e Ask students to compare Jesus' eight sentences with their own. Are there any similarities? What differences can they find? Talk about what difference it makes to use the word 'blessed' instead of 'happy'. (Christians might say that it is because happiness is a gift of God rather than a human achievement.)

f Ask students to take one of Jesus' eight sayings and make a cartoon or a drawing to show what it means.

Jesus' eight sentences for a happier life

Blessed are the poor in spirit,
  for theirs is the kingdom of heaven.

Blessed are those who mourn,
  for they will be comforted.

Blessed are the meek,
  for they will inherit the earth.

Blessed are those who hunger and thirst for righteousness,
  for they will be filled.

Blessed are the merciful,
  for they will be shown mercy.

Blessed are the pure in heart,
  for they will see God.

Blessed are the peacemakers,
  for they will be called children of God.

Blessed are those who are persecuted because of righteousness,
  for theirs is the kingdom of heaven.

Matthew 5:1–10, NIVUK

A simplified version

You are happy if you rely on God, not yourself: God's kingdom belongs to you.

You are happy if you wish things were better: you will be comforted.

You are happy if you think you are low down: God will give you all the Earth.

You are happy if you long for justice: one day you will be satisfied.

You are happy if you are full of mercy: others will then show mercy to you.

You are happy if your heart is pure: you will see God.

You are happy if you make peace: you will be known as a child of God.

You are happy if you are picked on for doing good: God's kingdom belongs to you.